Healthy Eating

Sweets and Snacks

Susan Martineau
and Hel James

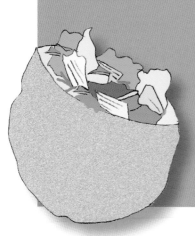

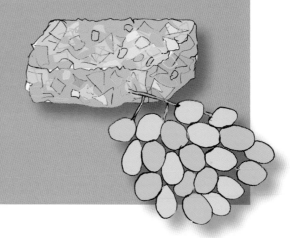

A⁺

Smart Apple Media

Published by Smart Apple Media
2140 Howard Drive West, North Mankato, MN 56003

Designed and illustrated by Helen James
Edited by Jinny Johnson

Photographs: 10-11 Owen Franken/Corbis; 12 Bob Krist/Corbis; 13 Ed Young/Corbis;
16 Envision/Corbis; 18 George D. Lepp/Corbis; 19 M. ou. Me.Desjeux,Bernard/Corbis;
20 Richard T. Nowitz; 22 Gary Houlder/Corbis; 24 Pitchal Frederic/Corbis Sygma;
26-27 Ludovic Maisant/Corbis.
Front cover: Ralph A. Clevenger/Corbis

Printed in Thailand

Library of Congress Cataloging-in-Publication Data

Martineau, Susan.
Healthy eating. Sweets and snacks / By Susan Matineau.
p. cm.
Includes index.
ISBN-13: 978-1-58340-897-1
1. Dessert—Juvenile literature. 2. Snack foods—Juvenile literature. I. Title. II. Title: Sweet and snacks.

TX773.M277 2006
641.8'6—dc22   2006014440

First Edition

9 8 7 6 5 4 3 2 1

Contents

Food for health

Our bodies are like amazing machines.
Just like machines, we need the right
kind of fuel to give us energy and
to keep us working properly.

If we don't eat the kind of food we need to keep us healthy, we may become ill or feel tired and grumpy. Our bodies do not like it if we eat too much of one kind of food, such as cakes or chips.

We need a balanced diet. That means eating different kinds of good food in the right amounts.

You'll be surprised at how much there is to know about where our food comes from and why some kinds of food are better for us than others. Finding out about food is great fun and very tasty!

Can we go to the candy store now?

A balanced meal!

The good things, or **nutrients**, that our bodies need come from different kinds of food. Let's look at what your plate should have on it. It all looks delicious!

Rice, bread, and pasta

These foods contain **carbohydrates** and they give us energy. They are also called starchy foods. About a third of your food should come from this group.

Fruit and vegetables

Rice, bread, and pasta

A juicy peach is a great snack.

Fruits and vegetables

These are full of great **vitamins**, **minerals**, and **fiber**. They do all kinds of useful jobs in your body to help keep you healthy. About a third of our food should come from this group.

Milk, yogurt, and cheese

These dairy foods give us protein and **calcium** to make strong bones and teeth.

Meat, fish, and eggs

Protein from these helps your body grow and repair itself. They are body-building foods. People should eat some of them every day.

Sugar and fats

We only need small amounts of these. Too much can be bad for our teeth and make us fat.

Milk, yogurt, and cheese

Sugar and fats

Meat, fish, and eggs

Water

We need to drink at least six glasses of water every day.

Sugar and fat attack!

Candy is full of sugar. Sugar gives us a quick burst of energy but doesn't have any healthy nutrients. Too much sugar is bad for your teeth.

Some of the other snacks we eat, like fries and chips, are full of fat and sometimes very salty. Too much fat and too much **salt** are not good for our bodies. Cookies and cakes can be nice to eat, but they are also very fatty. We do need some fat in our balanced diet but not too much!

Should I buy a bag of candy today?

Try and think about a balanced meal when you are choosing a snack. Swap your fries for some plain popcorn or grab a piece of juicy fruit instead of a bag of candy.

Everyone likes to eat candy sometimes, but it's best for your body to choose healthier snacks.

9

Sweet stuff

It is hard to say "no thanks" when your friends offer you candy. There are so many different kinds of candy in the stores to tempt us, but they are all made with lots of sugar. We need to be careful not to eat too much candy.

Your teeth don't like it when you eat too much candy. Hard candies, like lollipops, take a long time to eat, and it is like giving your teeth a bath in sugar. This gives **bacteria** a chance to make **acid** that attacks your teeth!

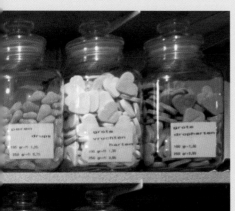

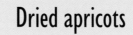
Dried apricots

Have some fresh or dried fruit instead of candy. It is full of vitamins and minerals. Dried apricots and raisins give your body **iron** that is good for your blood.

Raisins are dried grapes.

Grapes are a great snack, too.

Take care of your teeth by cleaning them twice day.

Chocolate

Chocolate is made from cocoa beans. These beans are the seeds of the cacao tree that grows in South America and Africa. The cocoa beans grow inside large pods on the tree.

When the beans are taken out of the pods, they are dried and roasted. Then they are taken to factories where they are used to make many different kinds of chocolate.

There is a lot of fat and sugar in chocolate. It is best not to eat it every time you have a snack.

Dark chocolate has iron in it, but it still has lots of sugar and fat, too!

Cakes, buns, and cookies

Eating a cake or some cookies for your snack is all right from time to time, but cakes, buns, and cookies contain a lot of fat and sugar. Look at the labels on the packages the next time you are in a supermarket to find the sugar and fat content.

The body needs a bit of fat to help it grow and to use certain vitamins. The best type of fat for the body comes from nuts, seeds, and oily fish; not from cookies and buns!

After school, snack on some breakfast cereal or a pile of breadsticks dunked in your favorite dip.

Humus and breadsticks

Eat some fresh fruit like a banana or a bunch of grapes instead of a cookie. Your body will love all of the vitamins in them.

If you want cakes or cookies, try making your own. That way you know exactly how much fat and sugar is in them.

Make cakes with healthy oats.

Make muffins with whole wheat flour.

Ice cream and Popsicles

Ice cream is made from milk, cream, and sugar. It can be made at home, but most of us eat ice cream that has been made in factories. Many kinds of **flavorings** and colors are added to the ice cream.

The mixture is stirred in huge vats as it is being frozen. Chunky **ingredients**, like fudge or nuts, are mixed in later. What is the weirdest ice cream flavor you have ever tried?

Ice cream is a tasty treat, but it has lots of fat and sugar in it. It's best not to eat too much ice cream.

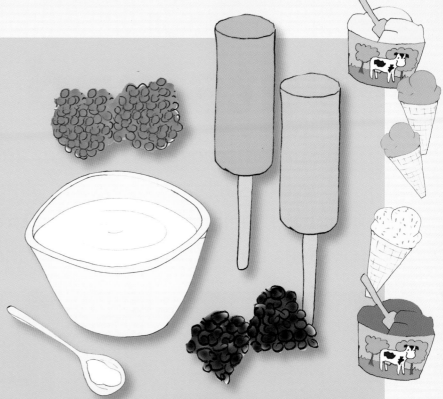

Yogurt can be frozen too, but the store-bought ones still contain lots of sugar. Try making your own with plain yogurt and fresh fruit.

I have an orange Popsicle!

Popsicles from the supermarket have lots of sugar in them. Try making some at home using fresh fruit juices.

Nuts and seeds

Nuts and seeds grow on trees and plants. The nuts we eat, such as pecans and almonds, grow inside a hard shell on the tree. We can eat some kinds of seeds too, such as sunflower and pumpkin seeds.

Almonds

Nuts and seeds have fat in them, but it is the type of fat that is better for our bodies than the fat in snacks like cakes or fries. It is called **unsaturated** fat.

Pistachios

Walnuts

Peanuts do not grow on trees. They grow in pods under the ground. That is why they are also called groundnuts.

Nuts and seeds contain protein, vitamins, and minerals to help our bodies grow. They are good for vegetarians who do not get their protein from meat.

Sesame seeds

Watch the salt!
Too much salt is not good for us. Always check that the nuts and seeds you choose have not had lots of salt added to them.

Sunflower seeds

Pumpkin seeds

Chips and salty snacks

The next time you go to the supermarket, try to count all of the kinds of chips and salty snacks you see. It could take you a long time!

Chips are made from thin slices of potato that are fried in big tubs of oil. Then they are put into large, turning drums and sprinkled with different flavorings and salt.

Some salty snacks, like tortilla chips and corn puffs, are made from corn. They come in many shapes and flavors.

These snacks contain fat and lots of salt. If you pack some in your lunchbox, balance them with healthy foods, such as fruit or yogurt and a healthy sandwich.

Raisins

Walnuts

Pistachio nuts

Pumpkin seeds

Almonds

Sunflower seeds and sesame seeds

My snack mix

Have fun with your friends and make up your own snack mix. Pop some popcorn and then mix it with raisins, unsalted nuts, and seeds.

Fries

French fries are made from potatoes. Potatoes are a good energy, or carbohydrate, food, but fries are made with lots of oil. They pack a lot of fat!

Did you know that thinly-cut fries are worse for you than thick fries? This is because thick fries do not soak up quite as much oil as the thin ones.

Eating fries every now and then is all right as long as you are also eating lots of healthy foods, such as fruits and vegetables. Having fries every day is loading up your body with lots of fat that can make you unhealthy as you grow up.

What do you like on your baked potato?

Get your carbohydrates from a baked potato, rice, or pasta instead of fries.

Sweet corn and tuna is good, but I like cheese and beans, too.

Pizzas and pies

Pizzas and pies make a tasty snack but they are **processed** foods. This means that they have had many different things done to them to make them ready for us to eat.

Pizzas bought from supermarkets are made in factories.

Freshly made food is much better for us than food that has been through many different stages in a factory. It has more vitamins and minerals in it. Processed food often contains too much fat, sugar, and salt.

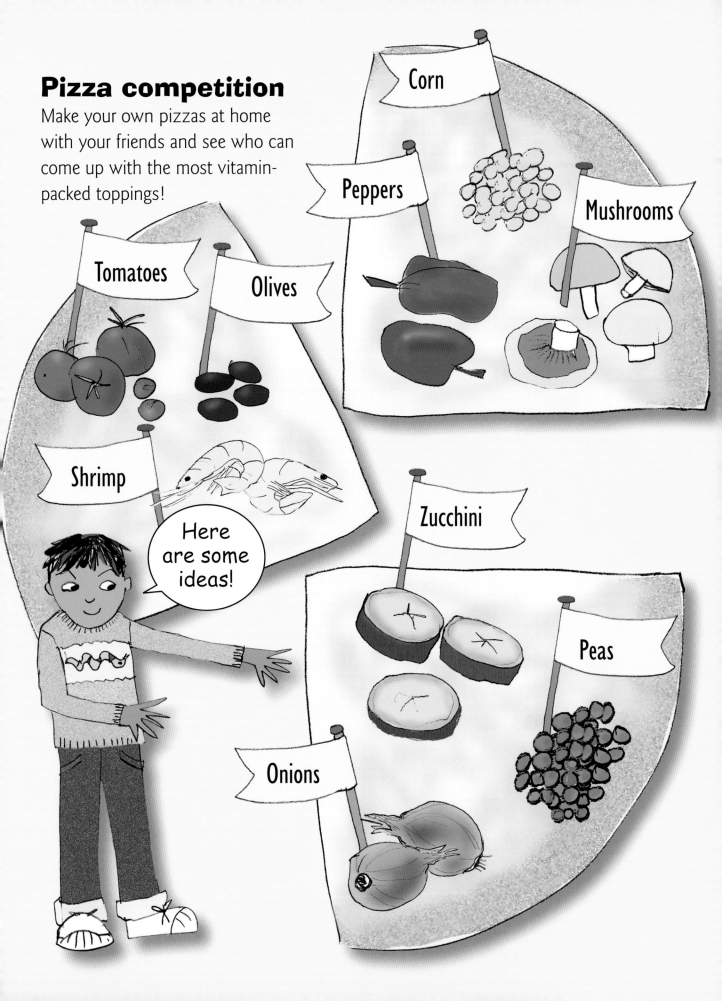

Fast food facts

Fast food is food that is made quickly and served up fast! Some of it is not very healthy. Look for fast food that will be better for you. Try to choose sandwiches, wraps, and salads that have good nutrients for your body.

Burgers, hotdogs, and chicken nuggets are some favorite fast foods. They are not made from the best meat. Many other things have to be added to it to make it taste better.

These fast foods are very processed foods. They are full of fat and salt and do not give your body the nutrients it needs.

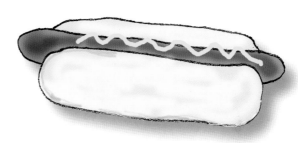

Chicken and lettuce on a roll is much better for you than a hotdog.

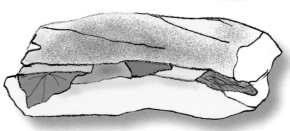

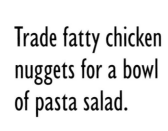

Trade fatty chicken nuggets for a bowl of pasta salad.

Make your own fast food

If you make your own fast food, you will know exactly what ingredients have gone into it. You can also cook it without using extra fat or oil. Always ask an adult to help you when you are cutting things or using the oven.

Wash your hands well before starting to cook.

Pocket a salad

Cut some pita bread open and stuff it with a delicious salad, cheese, or cooked chicken.

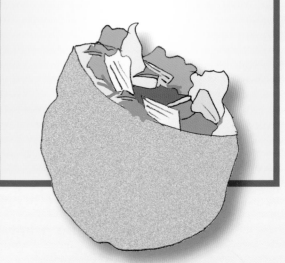

Nicer nuggets

Cut up some chicken breast. Dip it in beaten egg and then breadcrumbs. Bake the nuggets in the oven until they are crispy.

Add some herbs or spices to the breadcrumbs to make chicken nuggets extra tasty.

Have a healthy day!

Real burgers

Mix some **lean** ground meat with chopped onion. If you like, add chopped herbs and a bit of pepper and a little salt. Squish into burger shapes. Then grill the burgers until they are done.

Words to remember

acid   Acids are sour-tasting liquids. Lemon juice and vinegar are acids. Acid is made when bacteria eat the sugar in your mouth. This acid then starts to eat into your teeth!

bacteria   Tiny creatures that are so small we cannot see them. Some bacteria are good for us, like the bacteria in yogurt; some are bad for us and can make us ill.

calcium   A mineral that helps build healthy bones and teeth. Dairy foods, like milk, yogurt, and cheese, have calcium in them.

carbohydrates   These are the starches and sugars in food that give us energy. Carbohydrate foods are rice, pasta, bread, and potatoes.

fiber   Fiber is found in plant foods like grains and vegetables. It helps our insides work properly.

flavorings   These are added to foods to change the way they taste. Some flavorings are natural, such as herbs and spices. Other flavorings are man-made. Processed foods often contain lots of flavorings.

ingredients   Different foods that are mixed together to make something we can eat.

iron   A mineral in food that we need to keep our blood healthy.

lean   Meat without fat.

minerals   Nutrients in food that help our bodies work properly. Calcium and iron are minerals.

nutrients   Parts of food that your body needs to make energy, to grow healthily, and to repair itself.

processed   Many foods are processed which means they go through some changes before they reach your plate. Some foods are more processed than others. Fast foods and ready-made meals are usually highly processed.

protein   Body-building food that makes our bodies grow well and stay healthy.

salt   Salt has been used for hundreds of years to make food taste better, but too much salt can make your heart unhealthy when you are older. There is a lot of salt in processed and fast food.

unsaturated   Unsaturated fat is the kind of fat that is found in vegetable oils, nuts, seeds, and oily fish. It is better for you than saturated fat which is found in cakes, cookies, pies, ice cream, chocolate, and many processed foods.

vitamins   Nutrients in food that help our bodies work properly.

Index

Web sites

Learn which foods make a healthy heart.
http://www.healthyfridge.org/

Test your nutritional knowledge with quizzes, dietary guidelines, and a glossary of terms.
http://www.exhibits.pacsci.org/nutrition/

Find out how to have a healthy diet without eating meat.
http://www.vrg.org/family/kidsindex.htm

Get the facts about fast food restaurants and tips for making healthy choices.
http://library.thinkquest.org/4485/

Take the 5-a-day challenge and learn about fruits and vegetables with puzzles, music, and games.
http://www.dole5aday.com/

Discover ten tips for a healthy lifestyle.
http://www.fitness.gov/10tips.htm